SOME HABITS

SOME HABITS
C. VIOLET EATON

OMNIDAWN PUBLISHING
RICHMOND, CALIFORNIA
2015

Original cover art: *The Enemy Amongst Us* by Ronald Lockett
(50" x 53" multimedia sculpture)
Photo: Stephen Pitkin/Pitkin Studio,
courtesy of Souls Grown Deep Foundation.

Cover text set in Univers LT Std & Adobe Jenson Pro.
Interior text set in Adobe Jenson Pro.

Book cover and interior design by Cassandra Smith

Each Omnidawn author participates fully in the design of her or his
book, choosing cover art and approving cover and interior design.
Omnidawn strives to create books that align with each author's vision.

Offset printed in the United States
by Edwards Brothers Malloy, Ann Arbor, Michigan
On 55# Heritage Book Cream
Acid Free Archival Quality Recycled Paper

Library of Congress Cataloging-in-Publication Data

Eaton, C. Violet, 1982-
  [Poems. Selections]
  Some habits / C. Violet Eaton.
      pages cm
  ISBN 978-1-63243-004-5 (pbk. : alk. paper)
  I. Title.
  PS3605.A856A2 2015
  811'.6--dc23
                          2014040739

Published by Omnidawn Publishing, Richmond, California
www.omnidawn.com   (510) 237-5472   (800) 792-4957
          10 9 8 7 6 5 4 3 2 1
          ISBN: 978-1-63243-004-5

the church is near but the path is icy

the tavern is far but we shall walk carefully

(Russian Proverb)

I

Dear David,

Closed like a system, night sounds off : hounds bay, cicadas drone, wampus chuffs like a hog. Sparrows are hovering over the interior belt. they get tall. they chirp : *welcome to our nervous vespers.* A lot of us are here within it. down in the texture.

Were I not got half a heart so fits.

I discovered this morning upon waking that I did get a good drunk or so out of my weekend. a good page too : that's from the notebook. I work both into the text, slowly, altering for sound or for rhythm, listening through the form & into the space the blood hits.

In the distance the whine of an ATV echoes, emanates upward, gets in the head like butane. How can you see. Nimbus borne up, loud like a filament, tonal. A jay. Wasp. Smallish twinkle of glass among gravel. The atmosphere which is off-white, nearly duskcolored though day. Pumpkins rot. Toads. Out by the Old Wire Road a thresher sleeps, end to the furrows : shewes its mass. The cassette lurches & slurs.

My dearest friend I cashed three checks last week. Some little money on its way to you. For a limb needs a sleeve. & nothing is less certain.

I can think of no other way.

I found the mark of carbon in your last letter

& sound colliding. The cassette barking a mess in the day. Two radiators dueling along the taut line of my dwellingplace. One refrigerator kicked. To put some rhythm in.
How you can see. The terrestrial world, bound by geomorphic features, resembles a proscenium. From the porch the eyeline is divided by the hill, as each man is divided, for the devel is in his brest & revith hym the beleve. Even here, near the screen door, the thermal signature seems different, as it were, comyng oute of the eire.

A closer look reveals this vague incarnadine glamor

faint lights which notwithstanding their moderate luster give an impression of a white or at the most of a light yellow appearance on the retina : circular frame engaging ochre : mute : dropped back from those shadows : almost in light separate from the eye's aspect : the willow stippled by antlers

the hydrogen then the oxygen coupling : variegated star spreading outward : light upward in a line tensing violet then white then white again : puce : smallish streak of yellow pushing pale to the treeline : what mirrors myself in passing : myself makes of pasture a point refracted : a point there in space

where the slow crucible of sight catches : in the lower right corner of the margin : a line (almost) visible there pitched upwards : such as myself knows : if water can be counted for its sides & angles : if it smells of watermelon it must be the premonition of snow is carried inside & even so

Over the hill, the pond stokes the wheel. Where is produced the 60Hz hum. Where I sleep when it is warm.

I can call us complicit, or I can sit here on the porch and worry on us, hard. Neither thing is there. The hum is there.

The hum washed out, compounded by what was spoke. The hum beating against C#min9.

Will you quit me. Will our house dissolve. Won't water croon as it lets from the joist. In just-intonation, too complex to sort.

Water in E.

Among the cedar brakes the daubers flit. Lord lord. Anxious to see them beat the devil out there in the millpond. One thing I anticipate. Hello o hell. In one of my dreams, he is teaching me how to wear this suit, how to shoot my cuffs.

So there's the adversary. & there's his horsey, pulling carriage.

I chink a bit from the southern wall, let the light through & into the mouth. I watch you that way, from the airy cage of my chair. While burning the pond off, you walked a purling crescent. It's a film about causality & you're in the establishing shot. You & whatever ribcage you've thrown against the wind.

: : :

In a later frame : verdant print, this hunter, Prussians. You paint yourself up to attract a better storm – one that never seems to come.

The human spirit is celebrated within the haptic pause. As such, the seasons wane. Months synodic, sidereal, tropical. The anomalistic month, the draconic month. The wolf interval of February in its quadrennial leap.

David,

My dreams are often difficult to remember. Toward the middle heat of each night burns a deep, textural dream. The house continually shifts : I become lost in it. A presence on the periphery somewhere, not truly malefic, though it threatens. It's no less than insistent. I never *see*, but *sense* it translated through certain acts : the lights blink on and off. Something moves.

I have to go through the traces of somebody who's absent, so I'm digging through jewelry, a collection of dolls, reams of inscrutable notes. Constantly I am turned around. Figures from my past : some very close friends, others I thought I'd forgotten, appear as allies, or as agents of the presence (it's not always clear). It has something to do with the work. But it is still confused enough to react to energies in adjoining rooms. & not to matter.

PICK A SURFACE TO GET ALL CUT UP ABOUT : the bark of piney trees or the worthless carapace of human witchery.

Once I had both. That's on the square. Now I'm left alone not thinking much, only occasionally a motionless noon of some heat.

I still finger the crushed bag of the alphabet & it makes me measureless. I do this to keep it from growling. & that's all right. You get it tight enough most anything'll talk.

: : :

but not from the least of motion.   far for which.   some without of these.   in the out of.   when & with that over.   like that is it released. yes indeed.

the up.   the & the between.   & the them.   of a.   the along for but through.   the up & the of.   the were complete.   the was & toward on. will with away.   o from.   off & every like among.   the against.   the out of with.   in.   otherwise done.   they many.   whose very their all.   with whose was.   or to back those names.

is it to him.   though it did not with that.   see.   we across.   those on why they.   refuse the.   come of that come us to of that.   & so within. are of most.   whether from them was some as is.   it also has its begins.   in a.   in an.   under our which unto there.

you ain't you for so long.   these would.   here.   beneath acting never of the us.   is it it is.   can be of that.   the me there which is.   letting out. it is bright.

{   143   157   5   73   93   312   134   }

Pass me the bad luck.

from the gaseous miscellany.

if this were happening by the sea you'd know sailors. You'd pick a city with a cave nearby.   You'd know drinks.
Already you drinks.

Goodness :   Mercy :   how like a young bird.
                                             stuck in the hole you grubbed.

That language as old as the pattern on this carpet. I slept again.   &

the hash cake swallowed in the dream makes it across to the other side
Can no longer enforce limit
The cagey reflection on the side of dream the author wills
sovran for limit
Limits witness who come to nose them out

The strange guest, as tall as you   the one
with the keen blade
                              that fling with that woman
The one night I walked thru hell
To where she set the dummy supper

        Pulse staggering behind my lids
Now that I'm awake
The sparrows give me names like Choke-ass or Susan

Dear David : Welcome it's an else waltz.
It's like an aura, faintly untuned.

HOW IT HAPPENED

Sometimes I'd starve a little just to write. Other times it'd be pickled
eggs & cold beer. For a while it was Spaghetti-Os warmed right in the
can on top of a hot stove (amen). It's all so hard, the image is denser. Like
say one pint of tar in an old skillet.

Lately I've been spreading bacon grease and cherry preserves on crackers
: I top them with a slice of jalapeño. I picture them all without eyes,
something radiant. And I guess this same problem it has always already
existed. has usually set up in me somehow. Each knob which owns one
pitch within mine cursive striate. bent knees index. mammoth roil. eggs.
bones.

HOW TO READ MY FIRST BOOK / when it appears, there's a trace

HOW TO READ MY FORTHCOMING BOOKS / candlelight napkin & lipstick

In deed. Which is the signal laid for the guest. Who is the visitor advances in the steps I have just left. As if the conscious mind is ever present. Like in the tale a boy throws a stone at a white dog only to see the animal split in two parts. Only to let the stone pass through. Whereby the dog fuse together again.

Always name a good dog
after a bad man

Such is the America of my work

Whereby it fuse together again: "My work is certainly interested in the collage" : yes : I'm sure I said this once : I was an educate once : no more : I hiss now like wet turf.

Back then. In this one house in Ohio some previous occupant had left an electric organ. The room I slept in was cold & I had many fights with a woman there. Rodents nested in the plaster. The poems became concerned with a presence inside absence : with residual volume.
To configure a peculiar chord : to open slowly the gate of the footpedal.

& so the work stuttered into the audible.

Also modified by the spaces between the walls it carried on & on & again flooding the organ even after.

david my Dear It's been ten years, it's been fifteen, seventeen. I try to write truth possibly. it cannot cohere. You have known this for longer I cannot longer pretend. The hurts impulse : the necessary failure predicates.

Someone keeps the vines cut to a foot of the hill & this will give substance to the hill I think & the roots will grow larger. This will prevent proud flesh. The roofshingles will lay flat & not cup.

HOW TO DRENCH. HOW TO SWING OUT IN THE SODS / well I know a little. see : there : in the grass a sack of melons : lemon jelly : bag of kittens. a sort of melungeon.

observe the green false geometric twig. open the throttle of your bicep. let the tether out. on that stage it can get louder, lower. the faces that mend with private distance.

palms turned up

& you :   the warm mark :
unchart

you is more want
their empty of me
they intaglio

I do not believe things are the way things are

things

I recall as a child trains passing in the thin space between houses : cube
steak : the external. A train is a made thing. The slow error of it. The self
is a made thing : error of self.
A brittle heart the blood rules. A stasis.

       beam   *ray*   *vein*

   word   resonating within the chest.

I recall a wet slip left on a twig. & why I return to the old family notes,
the torn album full of gentlemen. the steams hanged in the back room.
Wound casually dressed. & that drone of certain musics :
Deltic, Celtic & Carnatic.

{   16   78   16   324   }

In the world beyond the hilltops, I imagine myself a builder or a man of public commitment, but this is seen through the rind, as it were. No matter how many times I revisit The Dark Corner, how many times The High Wall, The Crooked Way, The Naked Kiss, there are still so many rain signs.

But all signs fail in dry weather : this whole month was darksome dry : the goosebone told the tale that soon became snake drought. All the gov't weathermen grinned like shits. They mentioned beliefe & some blood come with it.

desist : : programmoars   (I say to them)
All that pleasure in knowing
soft forth mandibles of rock
chamber circle sun We are brightened with

what little magick held
Errata

& Dear fulgor you sort of implied spirit called david

only that reverie
trace of you
can Load us on it

So : okay : pattern emergence is overrated. Choose between conjure or the empty petition. Between the sweet ladder of breath & the one sound we had incept voice. The Irish discussion and the critical lecture. the Irisch & their reels. Choose the principle dialectic or the unified field. The answer veils the question. Choose among the questions. Between the leaf and branch.

& a new leaf will erect, maddening
as it harbors the county

itself
a madder crest   *bonetrue, landward, like the county's arm*

                    landward   arm is

eloped with moss

so you'll think on it some

David I am trying to scratch into what are observations. Hollow out :
will write of them here.

TO WEAN YOUR STOCK WHEN THE SIGN IS IN THE HEAD HEAT
OR BOWELS WIND IN THE EAST YOUR ANIMALS WILL FRET FOR
A LONG TIME : I HAVE KNOWN OF COLTS TO NEIGH FOR THREE
MONTHS & CALVES TO BAWL FOR HALF THE WINTER. PLEASE TO
OBTAIN THREE NUMBER ONE BUCKSHOT PUT THEM IN A PINT
OF FRESH MILK FROM THE COW : BOIL UNTIL HALF PINT. THIS
WILL ASSIST THE EFFECTS OF SALT & SODA, FOR THE SALT IS FOR
PURGATIVE & THE SODA TO REMOVE THE GAS.

puccoon : horsemint : physic : flax
pupbag of bitchdog : tansy stiff w/ bran
asarum : triphyllium : geranium : oak
chimneysoot is balm for cuts, tho
bulletholes want silk

sevenbark : ninebark : sheepshit tea
acker fortis cure the etch, or
slug of kerosene

the black ant powdered, mixt w/ lard
will prod an infant slow to walk :
will jake the curses slow to take :
shall cut the verses to the quick :

the dropper / the bottle / the bullet / the lug
'61 richebourg in a thunderbird jug

HANG IT IN
Radio theater. The two-hour call-in show blasted with fits of Wagner.
Public broadcasting. Thing which is elucidated. Slouch hat kept as
souvenir. Telephone company I paid them in fat ingots. It stops it flashes
it thunders.
cold coffee. (meat & drink both).
                              David not everything we've done goes
out : some sit in crates : some bloody the kitchen with thir prints. Some,
supplied with shoes, sit wait on the broken steps. plate of congealed
pasta. the postman on his bicycle stops unwraps a canister. wrought
from thine own hand. a major episode. communication. revelation. these
contravene. impair. O friend.

if this book were your house & if I were up there in it & if I ate a slab of bread you shall eat too for I like to think I have put the jinx on.

how wrong this'll turn out.

look down in my glass : a miller moth has got in & stopped moving. well. we've all been in the brambles at one time.

the night still just a baby, our talk accretes & flickers. as if forming a rhetoric that goes no place but eventually transmutes to seed. the glove of prepositions : the small naked foal of vowels.

you accused him of being a "wallpaper poet." & you're right of course. but are there not also baroque pictures underneath, between the studs? & are they not unhinging from the wall between the white spaces there? can you not entrust his jar of rancid paste? the bleached-out skull (*P. lotor*) atop the perfume of his memoirs? do you thus deny the considerable fact of his flesh? the soupcan full of nails where an old tune once was?

EVRY UTTER MAN CLEPETH WITHINNE THE PRINCIPAL WORCHING MIGHT.

So doth a lityl worde of one syllable, when it is spoken or thought.

so on to that postcard of yours. on from roads. I'm just in from the tat parlor & can't decide : the grinderman's capuchin or that one good pic of Charlie. which is it. it is. is it the aphorist's spittle hangs from your jaw. when you patter. chant. when you unhorse word.
Speech is better than a name, I always say. & a good name is better than wealth. than midges on the cattle.

Than leaving. Than crossing a slough
Than an unscreened film
Than law
Than the sense of any hatred
Than a useable tool

Like a grimoire   Like a level

The True Grimoire originated somewhere west of Memphis. We distilled from this a seam of fuel. Taken, burnt, offered, exact. & so now I find myself here, waiting for palsy courage, the audience rustling in their jackets. Listen. Don't be an expert. Become lethal.

The closest town, craters in every steeperoof. The men of this place are dropping pronto. I knew two guys, both stiffs now. Bodies offhand we weren't equipped to investigate. One shot hisself, a .44 : the other hung up on the working line. Point is, David, they leaned into the angle, arms flying, like boys who'd never been in the game.
Think they've touched it by now.

             I slid into the library and wrote you again.

        At the long table by the window.
I was a little of it. a little.
Up until a few minutes ago, a sullen, pretty girl was sitting here too. Low-res image of some dead rapper on her sweatshirt. I wanted to free her from sentiment. But I was unsure in the moment that we were even perceived. She left without saying *I am going away now*. How difficult.

The scene itself was muted, as if through a soft lens : there was no girl. How could I be sure?

If I drew you a picture . . .

here's the father melting to ether

he's at the moose lodge   his hair's cut
he's suckin carps from the river
because the moon in the valley
last night it went
          1, 2, 3,   1, 2, 3   1, 2, 3

you were the 4   you threw shade
on that moon
& the 7s
they still throw the old hand magic

The night I heard about your father I was on my way out the door. I went to R's place. He didn't have much : churchpew pulled under the table, fermented 18thc couch. A Chinese glove, metal, fingertips embellished with spikes (this hanging from a thin nail). We sat, smoked. I told him, then we breathed a little into the cup of living.

The walls wore their red, uninterrupted.

"What view have ye of God?"
　　　　Predestination.
"What think ye of man in his first
erectitude?"
　　　　A few ready switches set beside the doorframe.

Through time, I acquire the decency of ordinary experience. Through time, rather heavy draped, as it were, with tapped amplifier tobacco, shaky pentagram, lichens, yellow tin of pomade. But then a sudden dilation : across the sky the shades of night　rangy and oncoming : the forms of rite come now to me, halting, with shimmering Cadillac clarity.

I found you there obscure, waiting for the concert to start, one aspect in two halves. Unshaven. Illegible. Almost no selfregard.

Dear David,

the cleft in your dinnerplate pockets a swift.

that pink on my kerchief is waltzing away.

at first I seen you standing   one aspect in two halves.

half adder half real healer.

what's more haunted by far.

at first I seen you standing.

or else up then out spreading.

a series of expansions & contractions.

this is the first instant.

after that I'm in the smoke.

I'm back again   I'm in the smoke.

& from the smoke I'll pull the card
we call THE LIVING PHOTOGRAPH

& you shall see it, I mean me – in it – me, clad in underwear & a blue
robe holding a photo of myself holding a photo of myself holding a
photo of myself in which I am absent. dead in one coil. one hung wing
of an arm dropped by my side, posture which has no approachable title.

we cannot know what is the drug what is the panic. are we superseded by one or the other. is there some originary star in the center by the small window that opens when my eyes close. how wind does move through it. we walk around with it, we walk around with the daily clangor of sunlight, which we take into us and carry around the rest of the day. I smell my skin & it smells like me & I am taken there in comfort.

the essential mystery
is
why is there something rather than nothing

it may NOT exist & then what
our bodies break open
all seamy locks and pendants that's what

I broke open clear enough & sent that feeling north.

when I touch the drug it's as if I'm dying & I want to say something. that's because there certain seems to be this voice & I have said it before. did that not even. please. your poetry affects my outlook. mimic in it. for two whole minutes. I am sincere in this. in our discourse there is a thing without purchase we cannot scrutinize. a vacant trance. but all she speaks in : so he has to catch himself up in immeasurable snares. ok. you don't monkey with the sermon.

: : :

David, my favorite thing about you is you're on the material plane, subtle and insistent, like an interval of rain thrumming softly. It occurs to me : in you Finally it will rain. This rain can abate itself or, if cold, form radiating plates which arrange themselves in order of greatest to least density. Occasioned in the pasture : was repeated in the wood. We go to that dark rest in the score to wait. Is a spell we are feeling. Out in the ampersand.

It's as if I send each letter and it moves
upwards in elevation, beyond
the six-rail panels with locking crossrails in one quadrant
of the lot my kin cut out the land company
for some ancestral tone 71.67 cents above the familiar
& sympathetic to the cassette leaking
its chordal bodies scintillant
                        transverse
under the doublepitch
roof   voiced in a weird key, undivided

I need to know
is it the sallow wisp   what works in the space
above the long hallway
just off the kitchen
w/ its magnolia veins taped to the cupboard

outdoors
the sun keels
hoving up darking pictures

~~in front~~
~~the fox he circles~~
~~like just a wee fox would~~

Come to now. Fasting for three days & four nights under the vault of sky. It wore a brassy hasp. Edges of farms mapped against its steady line. Contrails unthreading after the jet passed. That selfsame vault opened at its hinge. Could put you maybe in that : you were the sixth animal, some habit.

A low thought.

HOW TO ADDRESS THE THRALL OF THE NATURAL / begin my dozens : natural language turning part-vellum, nettled by lye. Floor cluttered with pine needles before someone swept. The act of divining means. Sear a portrait there. Like a gill of rainwater but in the exact same place it fell.

{   119   289   }

dear david frigid and highly frequent last night. made a list of every limit. smoked a pack of menthols for Kali, stick of boo for Robert Mitchum. Sir Richard Burton. Garcilaso de la Vega. drunk like a motherfucker. nary a lamp lit. half inch linoleum chunk in the pocket, soundless.

up to hock one. haul the rig & heave away.

ladies & gentlemens. the foul mammiform constitution which insults the mirror. when he disclaim. when he converse with others. when he himself in the water with a crooked head. hey. I'm at you. jerk. honky. thou art subtle and gross like the sun. obnoxious in four languages. for you I must invent a new type of disdain. that it would be sure to burn. dance monotonously around.

There is a block drift strewed over this wilderness.
Those high passes a dull grey after the switch.
Outward from this star, some myth.
The cult of the plectrum.   maybe.
The southborn scent.
As they administer the ceremonies at the ghats of Ouachita.
As I come I'm headless.
As I see I understand.
As I keep repeating.

   I keep repeating.

Yesterday I met a vapor from out the soil & he just stayed around.

What would that feel like wanting. Tongue drinking from inside a collarbone. Little cakes & fruits you ate throughout the winter.

Dear David : Imagine the viscosity of this connexion. In which no object is perceptible. In which a metaphoric engine : shimmering a ways though lilting in, headlit. In which the context disabuses itself.   Porous & destitute vision. In which the cassette ends.

View south from CR 41 & Signal Hill Road   Winslow, Arkansas.

Let's see is it   it is   is it   it is   is it

II

Hey. it is.
I keep winding up at this local bar to shoot pool, drink, and write.
The table's like a private garden   felted surface to powder the
                                                                  elements.
Raise cue   make sound   powder elements.
The repetition is what makes it.
On the 3rd, 6th, & 9th days I warm it with an oaken board.
A plank once stretched from roots to bowers.
The dudes approach   I wave them be   am no sucker.
They shrug & huff & slouch away I love them each.
My hatful of swell teen love.
I pot the balls one at a time, two if luck is with me.   press crank   poke.
Cut six games out quick.
Deliver whitey to the far rail & keep him there.
In the gutters.
In the wet tarp afternoon.
In the gutters, a triumph, a dirty creek.   mar twain.
When I drop two in the pocket I wonder did I see math.
Could it be the visitor.
Like, I have my dryads here alongside.
Or, "it were saten done it"   you know, the Telos.
Yon protopsychedele.
Either way.
There's all kind of truck on my lens.
Suppose I like a thick gravy but I love the immaterial gust better.
What then.
I give it up that's what.   I keep playing with my yellow earth nail.
The Articles of Confederation gloss this.
& our dead, glossed in equal measure.
Our dead are angry & unhappy with what we send up.
A simple deerhandle blade buried in the direction of wind.
The visitation will come from behind & to the right.
I lookd through the keyhole . . .
"A lurid light, a trampling throng / Sense of intolerable wrong."
I know the world will end march 1992.
Hup. cur.
Does it feel silent.
Wouldja swarm over as in dura, whiteness.
Didja get a taste yet.
Of the fantods.
The Indians not yet arrived.
We fear something amiss with our messengers or them.
The air is pure & helthy so far as we can judge.

But still colored in.
Of densest hue with dried erotic midtone.
. . . . & oil.
You are familiar.   famous.
Hey.
What are other things the mind already knows.
How to make public symbols.
Whether smearing code on a muzzy surface.
Or working a too-long shift.
I am reminded.
"To see is to forget the name of the thing one sees."
But it's still April.
So we drive.
The bald Mexican in the back seat w/ the bathsalts.
Hates me for counting.
Past the sign EL OOD APA TMENTS.
Past the sign BURIAL LOTS.
Past the sign 24 HRS A DAY COFFIN SALES.
Past the sign HATE SIN.
Past those chalkmarks on the plank-fence.
Those referents to devilment.
If I could leave the car I would measure them by hand.
& where my own hand fit I would mark with tape.
Total cross of tape.
This daisy in lucite.
The tiny chair.
It hovers while the flower is absolute.
I know how it is to be of it.
I know the sepal tints.
I know how I know she is there also.
She is making pictures of bats in my copy of *De anima brutorum*.
Where she smiles through the pinhole lens.
& gathers up her orange things.
Much intact.
She has just enough history that soaks.
It says much about we.
They.
If they are penetrated by the idea like chuckholes in the road.
They says you're curtains.
Well that's if they says some at all.
They says nothing.
Hay lodo.
Hay un lobo.

Dear David : November now : US 2 Yellow Corn Prices mostly down
2 cents for a state average of 5.43. Am sheltered in the glow of the back
porch light. Later, like a muleshoe, am to be set into the mortar at the
back of the chimney. For I steady regress. As it is, a ballad inscribed on
matter is I. & all of that now gone. & all shrove. Have often found myself
the confluent mass of humors the Greeks knew. & yet the work insists :
like you I have settled into the role of shepherd of these words.

                    & why not play the shepherd?
                    (he ask)

I will tell you david how to rid yourself of this melancholie : Bind the
entrails of a chicken to your left palm. As soon as the animal heat leaves,
drink good liquor. repeat for three hens. the whiskey kills the poison
while the chicken draws it out.

But we here speak of poems. A more precise metaphor is the rabbit. That music inside a rabbit which must be got. In this sense, the typewriter so like a piano : the modern form of which is credited to Cristofori, whose title was Keeper of Instruments.

My friend am keeper also : you shall know I possess these means. guarded therefore sacred.

the typewriter so like a   piano : a porcelain tongue worrying sulfate : magnesium : "de"-composition. it thresheth rabbit bone étude. IT STROKETH THE BLACK CUBE THAT IS ALSO THE WHITE CUBE. it reapeth from the void with giddy nitrous fist. in sheaves. & those fumes they sting the eyes. & these grip against the fold. quietly. sheaves to augment opens. breath opens. as trees do versus the washed-out hum. as kids sketching chalkforms in a dumbass Valhalla.

: : :

Or perhaps the harpsichord shall be the model?

But one must return to the organ

(this is not a metaphor)

Tallow or fiddlemusic issued from the organ

                                                    & in that one room
her feet kept pointing to the same place. which was down. *là bas*. the
room floating above the recess it was cut from.
& in the dimensions made reluctant, the woman would move. she'd come
along like school was out. arything else was just a stone sailed at the
water. a pons wrought of ash.

like the fungus that rose from your notebook

the lepiota what sprouted from your immense tower of poems

gomphus, tiny volva, myxomycotina

pink calocybe in fairyring formation

When I leave the medicine I have dreamed. When the water gets up out the river. When old thousand legs is toothless. When he's gettin it. When four men block the doorway. When it finally happens. When nobody said something to get up to. When I talk the bottle & whoop in it. When Ibid. 386. When the sun don't come up the same way. A difference in the quality of day, the chine of the ridge. When each war is a way of purging good light from our journals. When slow is the new loud.

When one man is playing the organ, another is stretching & nailing strings across the surface of a cedar box. When the room is uncomplicated mostly. When these tones slip through.
& for whom.
& when even then they touch light (brief) & cease meaning.

{   218   31   482   250   }

David,

The beer is warm but I cannot wait. It's too large a bottle & the form demands it.

I'm feeling a little restless. I put a Charlie Feathers record on. Charlie Feathers burns.

I did the dishes. I poured half that beer. I paced for a few minutes.

Went out put two from the .38 into the pond. Did I see math. Only this time weaker. Oblique.

Started back up the trail. Later in the pantry the pintcan of marigolds I come upon engenders some new crisis.

I inherit. Get over.

instead of. throughout. was also then. it didn't one with. at no about but still were. as to that, it would play. for them his it. on by. can against the along there. out of which a rim. brink. skirt. where is over. is it nearby that what is under. it is. how. huh. a how. thus whom. both.

afore all this, I'd been
rewinding the video of the ventriloquist in blackface : thot maybe I misread the monologue through the flecks on the track head.
no matter. to sup.
through food are formed breath and mind :
mush beans not doing the job tho, so : burnt a pit of rhubarb / passed the tocsin through my breath kiss & killed two. moved from speaking to intuition. wood busted. jaw harp twangin. rust hoop in the shed. small dried husk of turtle in the shed. husk beckons. call turtle. clap the dice against.

CUSS   why have you not often got down low david
& felt that pressure so it was worse
in the cut after that side walked

I have got real work to do

you got some real to you as well
like weak doo-wop :
dark,   driven,
gleaming drunk hundred
in the back of the buick
All my cash crossed up w/ snakedust
marked
& delivered to the stack wrapped in curses, oaths, payoffs,

those ordinary welts that might be human again.

they got me for operating an infernal Machine.
you know the one :
      the tyrant's foe / the people's friend. raise up my hand to it before
knocking back a mug of grievance.

& does this action reveal a flawed ethics? does it unmake us as icons? forgive me that I come down hard when you ask about meaning : I am rehearsing the complainte. words come in rivulets (this is one habit of mine) : I tell them to be less combinatory, rather to be dire and to sing in the manner of most molecules. O. as if it were suddenly in fashion, words, bot prively ment in the depnes of spirit. sully heap we can only grin at, clinging to the exterior form that's all.

the fire halfway between sun & earth I no longer doubt. not hellfire just a common fire. get out of that strange acre. you know. the one where you fall into manhood. I've already been & gone from. away. & to love. a man can a man cannot. my capacity to love is the Saxon guts of a tongue, until swallowed, growing cages & thrones in the heart.

if I were to guess, "he" (the heart) or "they" (thrones, loves) left the window open. so I saw some low clouds. no. a bare ass in the cemetery near the meadow. which approximates some of it. the rest, mere rebus on a gravestone. lain down. only halfthere. a collective of men standing in a greatroom. wind in retrograde.

: o david,

so you got loaded
I saw the clouds in your eyes

the thing is, we was bidden
immediately to form
          some volume of ignited gas
hereafter appeareth like a man
Not even this
benighted form of things

we love / we / wanted to make music that way

algid

                    & in one little space, with too many

what is anterior to the composition :

tonesmith inculcates the furthest pinprick

& in one little space, with too many. One's wildness like the white. Some
somewhat shadowed
particulate of light has to be.
                        We had already turned from the world so
we fail in that small way. The hollow world. THE HOLLOW MEAT &
FOWLS. some creepe into the caues of hollow trees. & this is where we
found the bones intermixt with branches :

HART HIND HARE BOAR WOLF

Each gone. all. I am sorry. The horse thief too has perished. I regret to inform you. slowing in the uncertain. cannot of. parse.

In Fludd's etching of the monochord a hand descends & tightens the peg. A constant motion deepens the flesh. It's the same when she plays an organ in her poem about organs : casting out from the plane of the page to touch it, every tactile sensation promised to visibility. NOLI ME TANGERE. The organ stops.

TIBIA PLENA, TIBIA CLAUSA   SESQUIALTERA, TIBIA REX

CONTRA DIAPHONE :   the quickness of speech

REGULA MINIMA,
TIBIA QUINT

AVICINIUM   twitters   as wind is admitted

VOX HUMANA   breathless   in its own swell box

it occurs to me :

you have your aggregate of modes

but if the universe is finite then the more I learn about the universe the smaller it becomes. I might say ignorance is a singularity. That's how not to see differentiation.

I've begun to hate this uncorrected cup of milk.
zooks
bitch
blaggard
Leave me & molt away. I hate your color, go away.

What I've become. & dull. & obsequious.

I've too much hate : too much behavior.
I'm not much for crowds.

The way bodies behave in crowds. The way a body behaves as a crowd.

The body which is contained as it passes, at every moment invading the larger curve.

I've too much body : too much knowledge. & so to you I pass over. Knowing. Wear this one. Here. Wear your tradition of fog. Your nametag. Sew it on your ancestral shirt. Keep in mind midnight. Keep overdubbed cricket there, within the chorus. Remember a glume a sheen. Observable phenomena. Think of a mountain to be moved through very (very) slowly as if you were not yet woke.

David,

I could call you Hiram you have solved the problem of loneliness   & I could call you Huddie you have set free your own inconsolable lot.

When I started you were in the city, a daily mission to reach & then pace the orderly stacks. That's yourself. To have a purpose, a cause. To be remunerated. I feel it though. For the ones who couldn't.

These days my letters arrive, drag you from your Carolina basement with the staggers & jags :

"Dear David,

"Do you remember with the weakest of lanterns telling bad jokes in the spire of the wood? It was good once. & we were there. seven bands on the bill. the drumkit you intoned once of. the levee you asked me to bring water from. your onetime stain cleansed by the thing that remained. the crown. I laugh. There we are.
"When we stop awhile in a certain place. & then walk on. only to turn & look at what we lit.
"OURSELVES WHEN WE ARE REAL.

Of course the real is where defeat is. & sometime summer clouds. Cluster
of horses afloat in the gloam. Which is the incarnation of sleep. wherein
flowers : 1,000 military marches sounded from the well of calyces there.
The horses flooding, gashed, white. Which is the provocation of sleep
: when the vital spirit throughout the body is discomposed. when part
has been forced out & lost. part compressed & driven into depths. limbs
unknit. grow limp. Like the city's on. but so is those off the old sweet
cracks.
Here come the water. the preacher say. whatever by these rains
is thus restored.

& *your* sleep should occur *here*, beyond the water,
through to the other side of the hills
where the theater of language emerges
One can't leave the boundary of this
lining a lavender dispatch away, cult girlhood :
I wear witches panties   & a loose paper dress

The garden is adrift.
Gavotte.   Chaconne.   Menuet. Mulch.

My sweet tall one
His is a very good painting   in it There are several dancers
& one plants on you a wee peck
Pudendum jutting out
the hem of her habiliment

She use that one crease. the sum of.

Another midground wears a dull face
in a patch of wet phlox
in her coalticked chiffon

. . .
: : :

"the garden is adrift" creates a cadence falls from lips. the rhythm a path
that meanders through a hidden grotto / it spans 15,000 irises 400,000
assorted bulbs the inside of which are draped with bells. to write is to
beckon order in this corridor. to make of corridor said drape of bells,
smaller, contained within the larger space. to make warm of distance.
what can profane. what can even kill. is it the bulb that hath so neat
escaped the cloche.

{   177   162   210   329   }

dear david there are still a thing which is vagrancy. i am convinced. you
are shivering outdoors, vernal, but you are a shroud. tho even shroud
should have its glossal sense. a certain glaucous pitch to this night : an
episteme streaked with gaslights : a sweetness.

dear david you are drowning at the edge of the grotto. in its bluish halo.
I can show you now. the dark quarter lit sudden with phosphor. how
many. hello. a flow of matter we watched down the path. we vessels
(I think). nouns to diminish. the long grass is our subtext. & we'll be
preserved. I will preserve you. the old you. & the current.

I cannot tell you. how we shall appear. in our acquired age.
what the place of refuge is like.
how many hits. how many seasons do you want.

Acknowledgements

A huge thanks to Forrest Gander, and to the incredible staff at Omindawn.

I also need to single out David B. Applegate, Kaveh Bassiri, Cody-Rose Clevidence, Martin Corless-Smith, Tim Earley, Jane Gregory (*thankyou thankyou thankyou*) & David & Opal Vandeloo, Whit Griffin, Matthew Henriksen, Kevin Holden, Myung Mi Kim, Cole Swensen, Michael Thomas Taren & Purdey Kreiden, Dennis Tedlock, Tim VanDyke, Roman White. Thank you all so much.

All the people I forgot to mention, whose books & existence I love & who come out to northwest Arkansas a few times a year to read or listen.

Thanks to Charles O'Donnell and Don Choffell for the greatest job in the world.

To my parents and my sister Emily, everything.

& to Sara Nicholson, you *are* everything.

A portion of this text appeared in *Fence*.

Some language from this poem was appropriated from, or inspired by, several other printed works:

> Richard Addington, *A History of Scott County, Viriginia*
> Anonymous, *The Cloude of Unknowyng*
> Anonymous, *The Lesser Key of Solomon*
> W.H. Bedford, *Fifty Years with the Moon*
> Samuel Coleridge, "The Pains of Sleep"
> Charles M. Doughty, *Travels in Arabia Deserta*
> William Ferris, *Give My Poor Heart Ease: Voices of the Mississippi Blues*
> Johann von Goethe, *Theory of Colours* (trans. Charles Eastlake)
> *Journals of the Lewis and Clark Expedition*
> Lucretius, *The Nature of the Universe* (trans. R.E. Latham)
> *Out of the Past*, 1947 film
> Vance Randolph, *Ozark Magic and Folklore*
> Abraham Rees, *The Cyclopædia, or, Universal Dictionary of Arts, Sciences, and Literature*, vol. 18

 C. Violet Eaton is the editor of *Bestoned* (a handmade journal of poetry) and *Rural Harmonics* (a 'zine), as well as the author of a chapbook, *No Outside Force Can Harm the Coyote* (Free Poetry, 2014). His work has appeared in *Aufgabe, BafterC, Cannibal, Colorado Review, Fence,* and the *Yalobusha Review,* among others. He lives in Arkansas with his wife, the poet Sara Nicholson, on the eastern bluff of the White River. He sells used & rare books.

Some Habits by C. Violet Eaton

Cover text set in Univers LT Std & Adobe Jenson Pro.
Interior text set in Adobe Jenson Pro.

Original cover art: *The Enemy Amongst Us* by Ronald Lockett
(50" x 53" multimedia sculpture)
Photo: Stephen Pitkin/Pitkin Studio,
courtesy of Souls Grown Deep Foundation.

Cover and interior design by Cassandra Smith

Each Omnidawn author participates fully in the design of his or her
book, choosing cover art and approving cover and interior design.
Omnidawn strives to create books that align with each author's vision.

Offset printed in the United States
by Edwards Brothers Malloy, Ann Arbor, Michigan
On 55# Heritage Book Cream
Acid Free Archival Quality Recycled Paper
with Rainbow FSC Certified Colored End Papers

Publication of this book was made possible in part by gifts from:
Robin & Curt Caton
Deborah Klang Smith

Omnidawn Publishing
Richmond, California
2015
Rusty Morrison & Ken Keegan, Senior Editors & Publishers
Gillian Olivia Blythe Hamel, Managing Editor, Book Designer,
& OmniVerse Managing Editor
Sharon Zetter, Poetry Editor, Grant Writer & Book Designer
Cassandra Smith, Poetry Editor & Book Designer
Peter Burghardt, Poetry Editor & Book Designer
Melissa Burke, Marketing Manager & Poetry Editor
Liza Flum, Poetry Editor & Social Media
Juliana Paslay, Fiction Editor & Bookstore Outreach Manager
Gail Aronson, Fiction Editor
RJ Ingram, Poetry Editor & Social Media
Josie Gallup, Feature Writer
Sheila Sumner, Feature Writer
Kevin Peters, Warehouse Manager